THE EASY PIANO COLLECTION
JOPLIN
GOLD

Published by:
Chester Music Limited,
14-15 Berners Street, London W1T 3LJ, UK.

Exclusive Distributors:
Music Sales Limited,
Distribution Centre, Newmarket Road, Bury St Edmunds, Suffolk IP33 3YB, UK.
Music Sales Corporation,
257 Park Avenue South, New York, NY10010, United States of America.
Music Sales Pty Limited,
20 Resolution Drive, Caringbah, NSW 2229, Australia.

Order No. CH74624
ISBN 978-1-84772-821-0
This book © Copyright 2009 by Chester Music.

Unauthorised reproduction of any part of this publication by
any means including photocopying is an infringement of copyright.

Edited by Jenni Wheeler.
Arranging and engraving supplied by Camden Music.
New arrangements by Jeremy Birchall.

Printed in the EU.

Your Guarantee of Quality:
As publishers, we strive to produce every book to the highest commercial standards.
The music has been freshly engraved and carefully designed to minimise
awkward page turns to make playing from it a real pleasure.
Particular care has been given to specifying acid-free, neutral-sized
paper made from pulps which have not been elemental chlorine bleached.
This pulp is from farmed sustainable forests and was produced
with special regard for the environment.
Throughout, the printing and binding have been planned to ensure a sturdy,
attractive publication which should give years of enjoyment.
If your copy fails to meet our high standards, please inform us and we will gladly replace it.

www.musicsales.com

CHESTER MUSIC
part of the Music Sales Group

London/New York/Paris/Sydney/Copenhagen/Berlin/Madrid/Tokyo

The Cascades
Page 8

The Chrysanthemum
Page 5

Cleopha
Page 12

The Easy Winners
Page 16

Elite Syncopations
Page 20

The Entertainer
Page 26

Fig Leaf Rag
Page 30

Heliotrope Bouquet
Page 34

Maple Leaf Rag
Page 40

Original Rags
Page 44

Palm Leaf Rag
Page 48

Peacherine Rag
Page 39

Pine Apple Rag
Page 50

Ragtime Dance
Page 54

The Strenuous Life
Page 62

Weeping Willow
Page 58

Scott Joplin

Born in Texarkana, Texas in 1868, Scott Joplin was central to the creation of 'ragtime'—a heady mix of syncopation and catchy melody. Initially seen as black music from the red-light areas and Vaudeville shows, it gradually gained respectability across America and reached Europe in 1900 when the band-leader Sousa, Joplin's white counterpart in American popular music, took arrangements of ragtime to Paris. Debussy and Stravinsky experimented with it in their piano music, and even Brahms intended to write a rag before he died.

Ragtime was a fusion of white marches and Western harmony with folk music and black rhythms from African drumming. In a piano rag the right hand plays off-beat melodies with a fluctuating sense of meter. This effect was difficult to master, and one early ragtime pianist called it 'playing two different times at once'. The influence of Sousa is found in the left hand, which imitates the 'oom-pah' bass-line of the march, providing a solid foundation for the syncopation above. The form of a rag mirrors the march, typically having four or five themes in two or more keys. Each theme is 16 bars long and repeated. Although ragtime was written to dance to, it is known from early piano rolls and recordings that *rubato* and exaggerated speed changes were an accepted part of its performance.

Joplin was one of six children of an ex-slave father and a free mother. He was given free music lessons in his hometown then left home, aged 14, and became an itinerant musician moving from town to town to find work. After working in St.Louis and Chicago he settled in Sedalia, Missouri in 1896. A quiet, thoughtful man, Joplin began to change attitudes among the 'respectable' classes towards ragtime. The 'sinful' syncopated music didn't seem so bad when played by this modest man. Gradually ragtime became popular with white people, which brought money and the chance for Joplin to publish his *Original Rags* in 1899. In that same year, publisher John Stark heard Joplin play at the Maple Leaf Club in Sedalia. Stark published the *Maple Leaf Rag* and with his financial backing it brought fame for Joplin, selling over a million copies across America.

In 1901 Stark, Joplin and his new wife Belle all moved back to St. Louis. *Peacherine Rag* and *The Easy Winners* were written in 1901, followed by *Elite Syncopations* and *The Entertainer* in 1902. Joplin tried to capture the sound of the tremolo style of the mandolin in *The Entertainer*. Also in 1902 he composed two marches, *Cleopha* and *A Breeze From Alabama*, still syncopated but retaining more of a march feel.

Relations between Joplin and Stark became strained as Joplin, against Stark's advice, wanted to try his hand at larger forms. He immersed himself in writing an opera, *The Guest Of Honor*, which was only performed once in 1903. The score was then lost and its whereabouts remains unknown.

Three rags from 1904 show developments in Joplin's style. *The Cascades* depicts the water gardens at the World's Fair in St.Louis, with left-hand octaves designed to sound like Sousa's trombones in its fourth theme. *The Sycamore* has a freer bass-line than usual and has some contrapuntal writing between the hands, while *The Chrysanthemum*, subtitled 'an African-American Intermezzo', is the first to have a contrasting, gentler mood in the trio section. In 1905 Joplin published his finest waltz, *Bethena*, which has five elegant themes in five different keys. The syncopation of a melody in 3/4 time gives a subtle effect.

After an unsettled few years which included a split from his first wife and the death of his second, Freddie Alexander (to whom *The Chrysanthemum* is dedicated), Joplin settled again in New York in 1907. He met and married his third wife Lottie Stokes, and in 1908 he published *Pine Apple Rag* and *Fig Leaf Rag*, as well as the instruction manual, *The School Of Ragtime*. *Solace* appeared in 1909, a Mexican tango-serenade full of romance and passion and in 1910 he wrote *Stop-Time Rag*, which incorporates the folk-dance practice of stopping the accompaniment and filling in the beat with foot stamps and slides. Despite the success of *Solace* and *Paragon Rag*, whose banjo-style trio captured the sound of the plantations, ragtime was in trouble. Stark's business was in decline as other styles overshadowed ragtime. Joplin and Stark finally went their separate ways and Joplin submerged himself in opera, this time with the three-act *Treemonisha*.

Treemonisha dominated Joplin's last years. He began to suffer mood swings, and although he staged one performance of the opera in 1916, he had neither costumes, props nor even a proper theatre. *Treemonisha* flopped and Joplin was crushed. His wife finally had him committed to an asylum and he died a broken man on 1st April 1917. Joplin's music remained largely ignored until the 1970s ragtime revival, which included a successful production of *Treemonisha* on Broadway and the use of *The Entertainer* in the film, 'The Sting'. Shamefully neglected in his lifetime, Joplin now stands as a creative genius who left a unique legacy of a truly American popular style.

Kate Bradley

The Chrysanthemum

Composed by Scott Joplin

© Copyright 2008 Dorsey Brothers Music Limited.
All Rights Reserved. International Copyright Secured.

Moderately

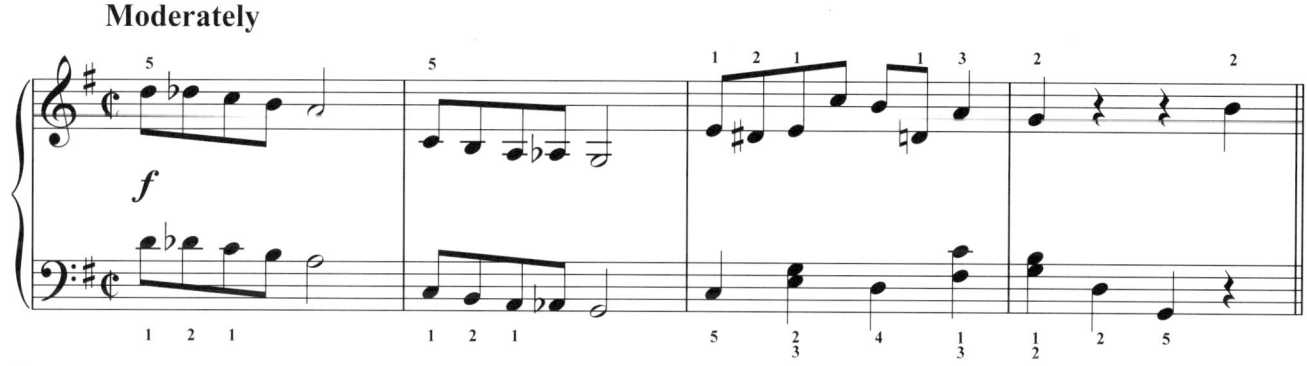

5

The Cascades

Composed by Scott Joplin

© Copyright 2008 Dorsey Brothers Music Limited.
All Rights Reserved. International Copyright Secured.

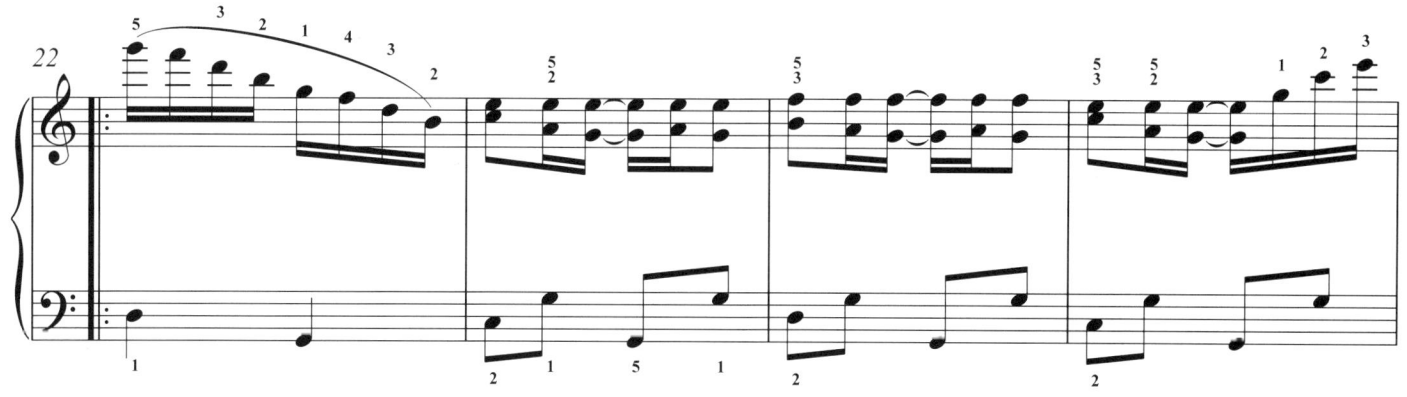

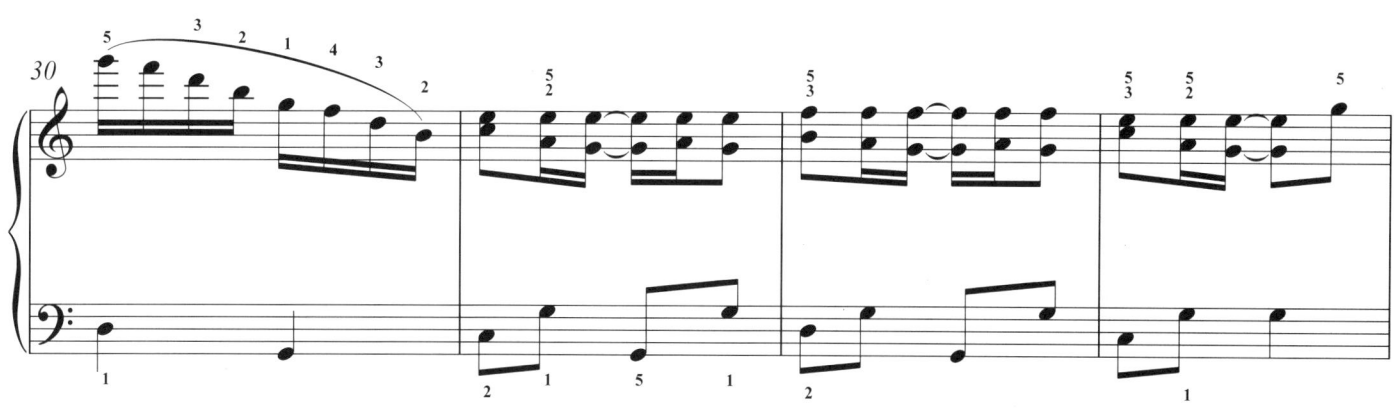

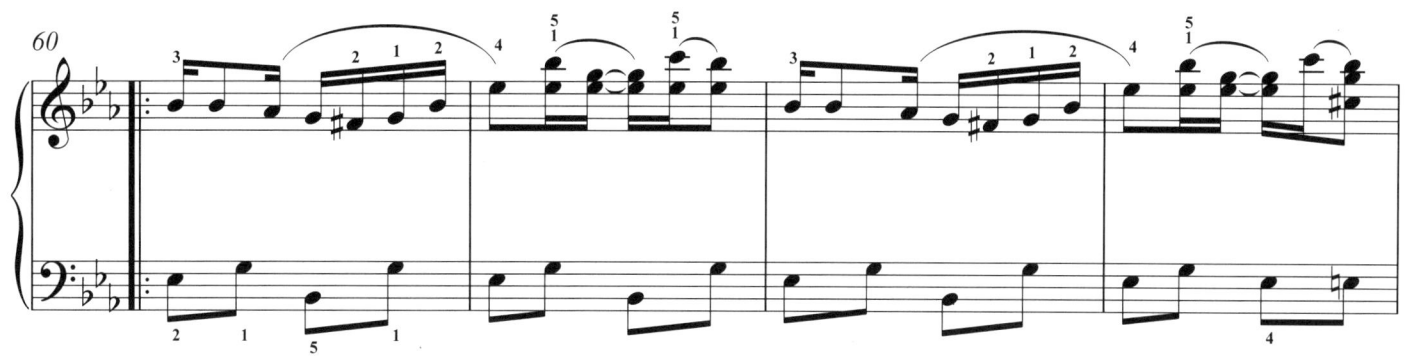

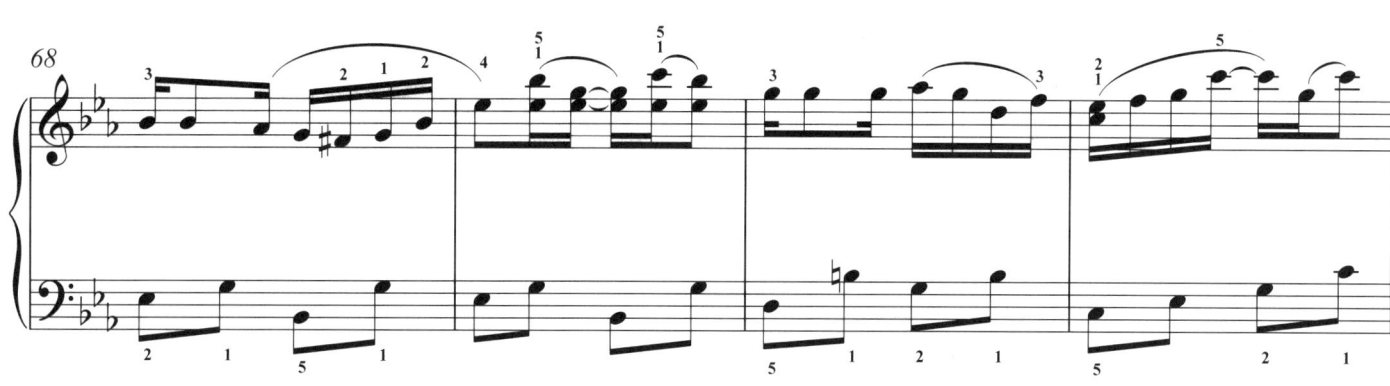
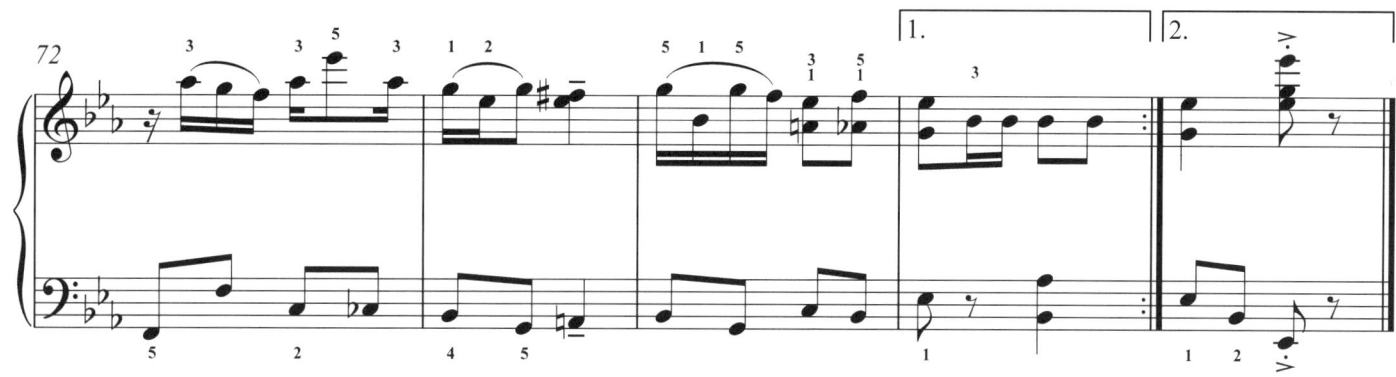

Cleopha

Composed by Scott Joplin

© Copyright 2008 Dorsey Brothers Music Limited.
All Rights Reserved. International Copyright Secured.

The Easy Winners

Composed by Scott Joplin

© Copyright 2008 Dorsey Brothers Music Limited.
All Rights Reserved. International Copyright Secured.

Elite Syncopations

Composed by Scott Joplin

© Copyright 2008 Dorsey Brothers Music Limited.
All Rights Reserved. International Copyright Secured.

Cheerfully and briskly

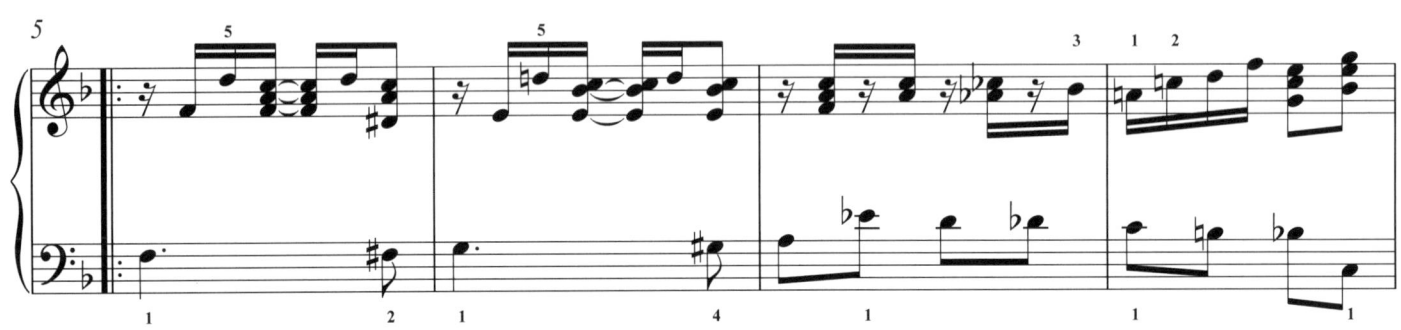

20

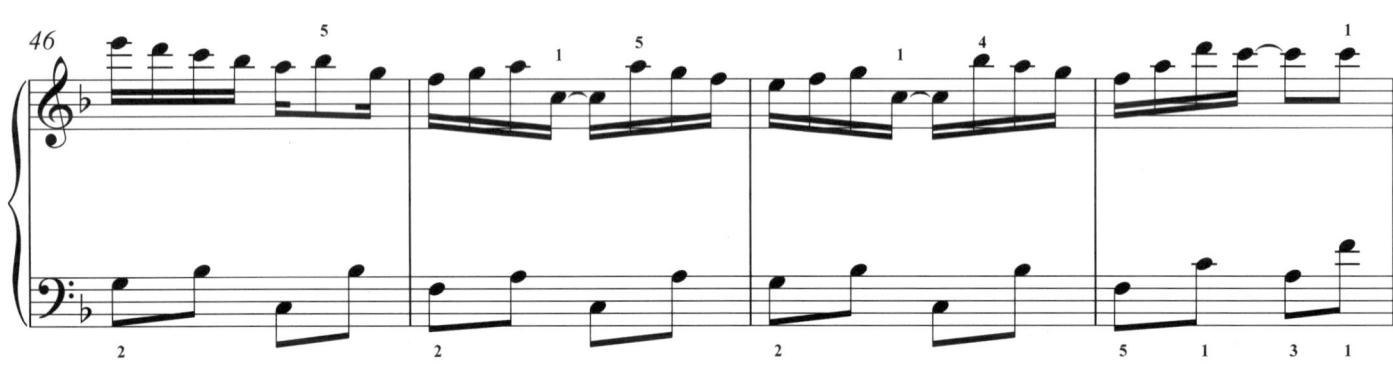

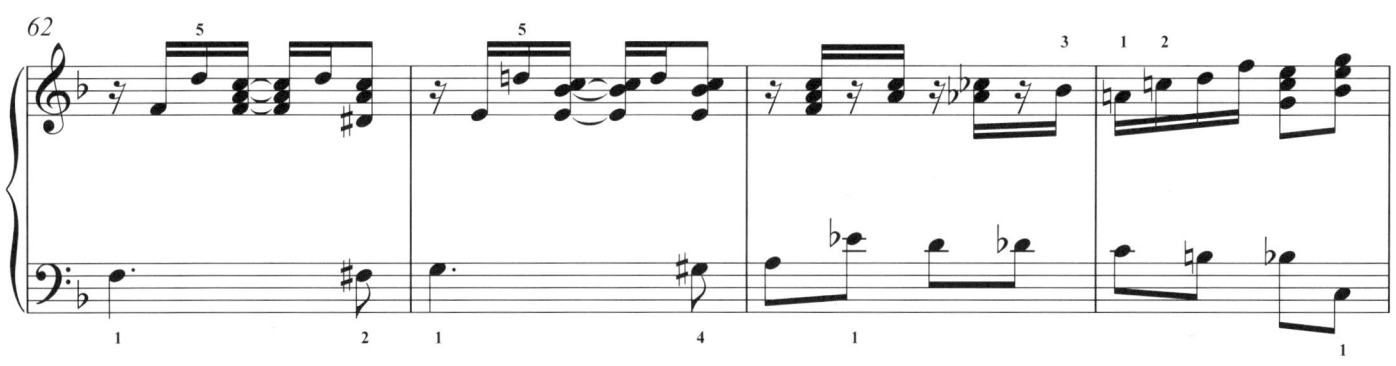

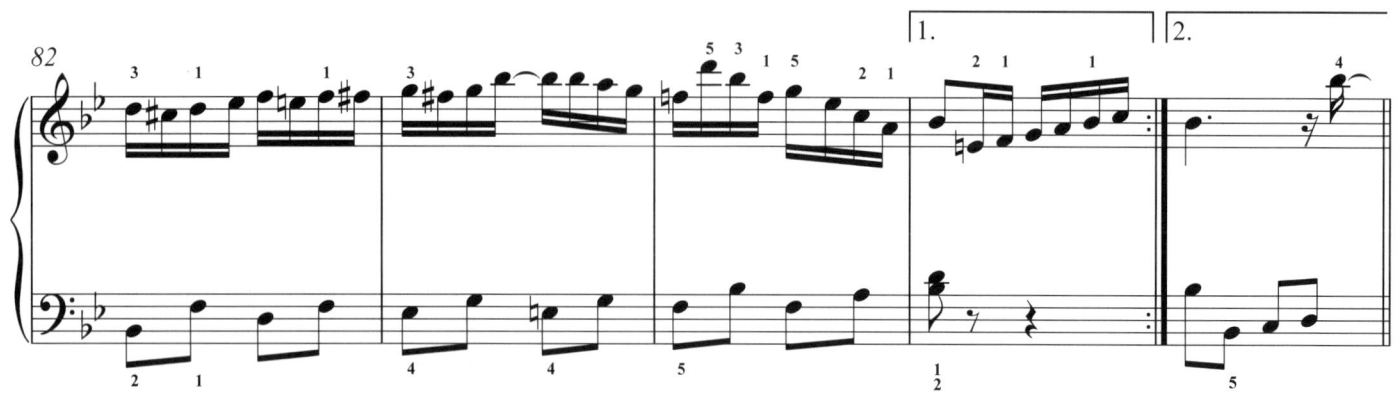

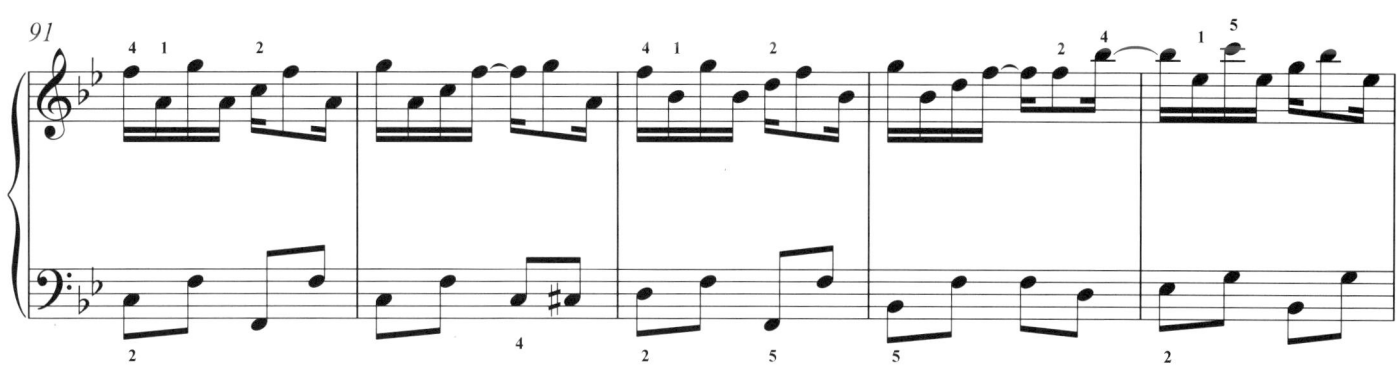
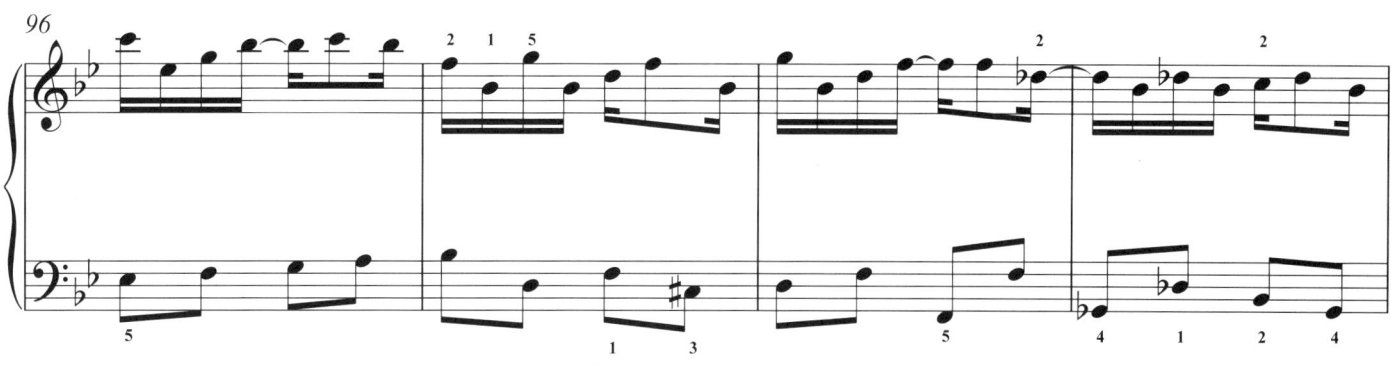
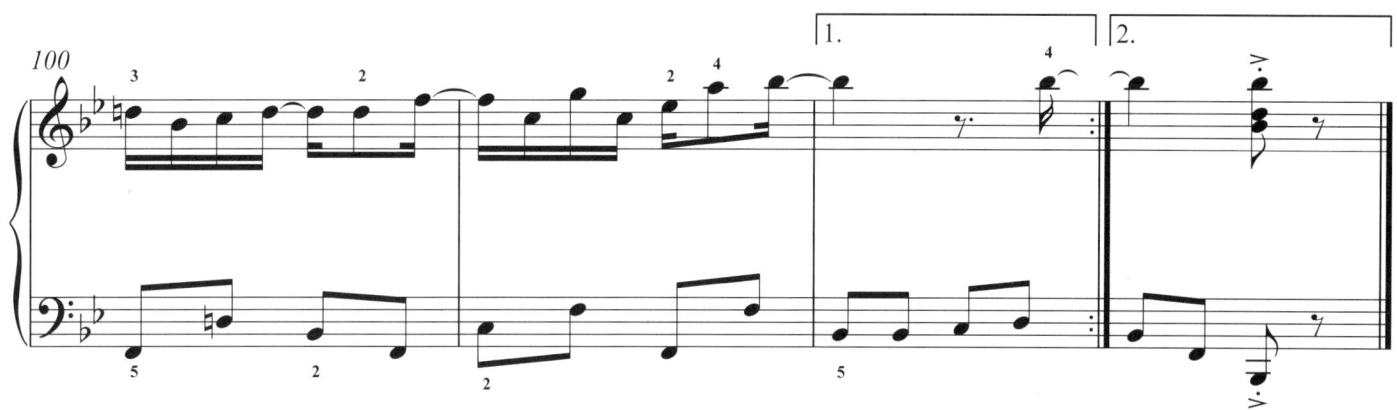

The Entertainer

Composed by Scott Joplin

This arrangement © Copyright 2007 Chester Music Limited.
All Rights Reserved. International Copyright Secured.

Fig Leaf Rag

Composed by Scott Joplin

© Copyright 2008 Dorsey Brothers Music Limited.
All Rights Reserved. International Copyright Secured.

Slow march tempo

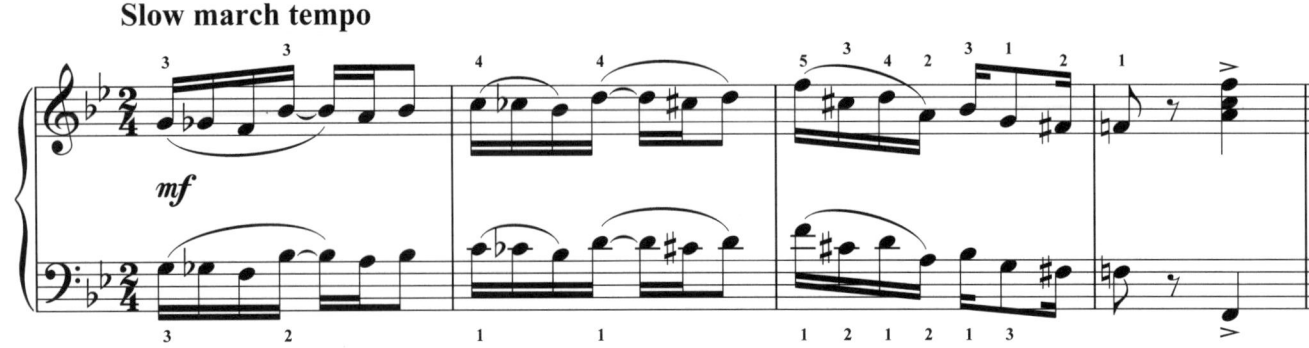

Heliotrope Bouquet

Composed by Scott Joplin and Louis Chauvin

© Copyright 2008 Dorsey Brothers Music Limited.
All Rights Reserved. International Copyright Secured.

Smoothly and steadily

35

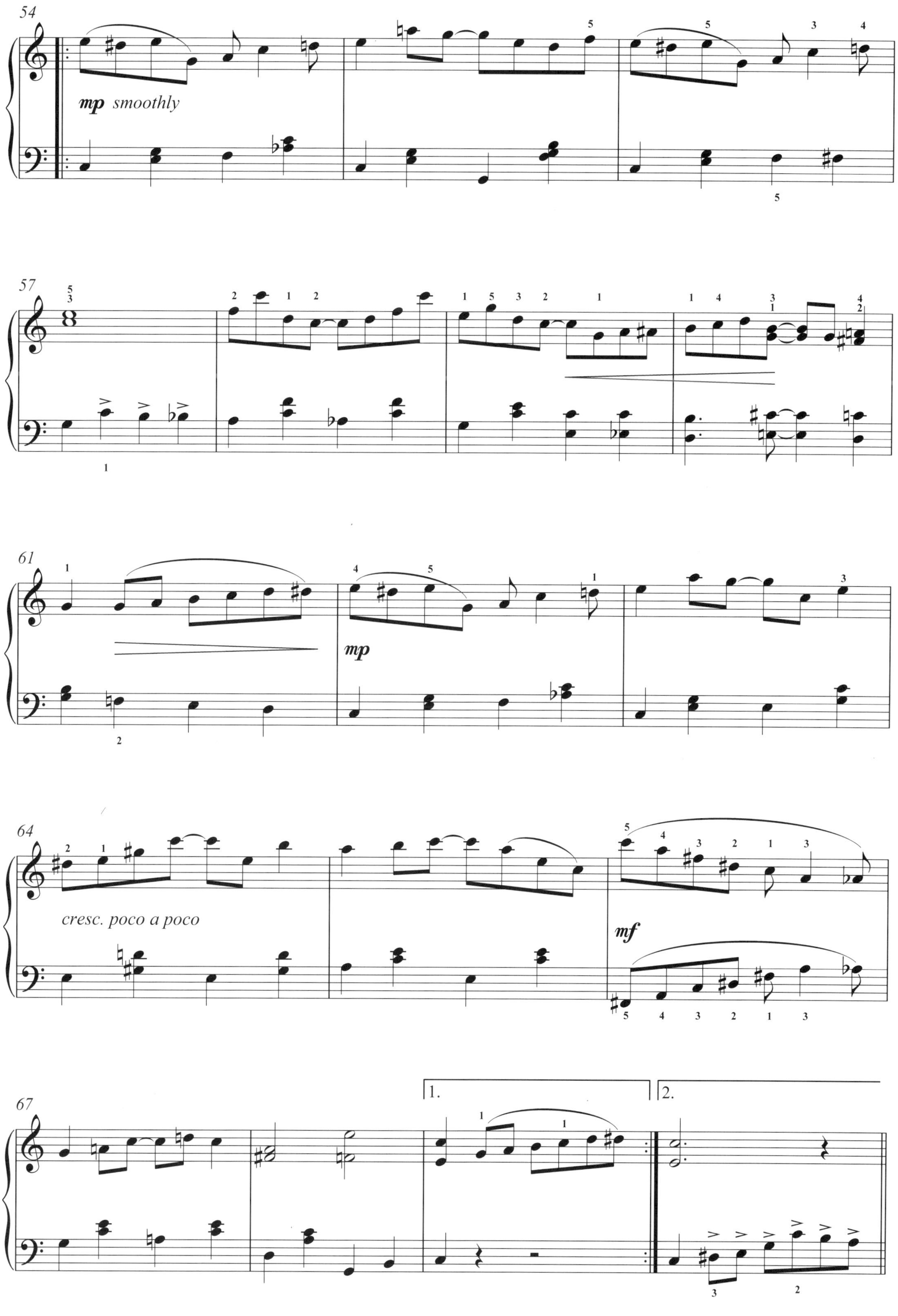
54
mp smoothly
57
61
mp
64
cresc. poco a poco
mf
67
1.
2.

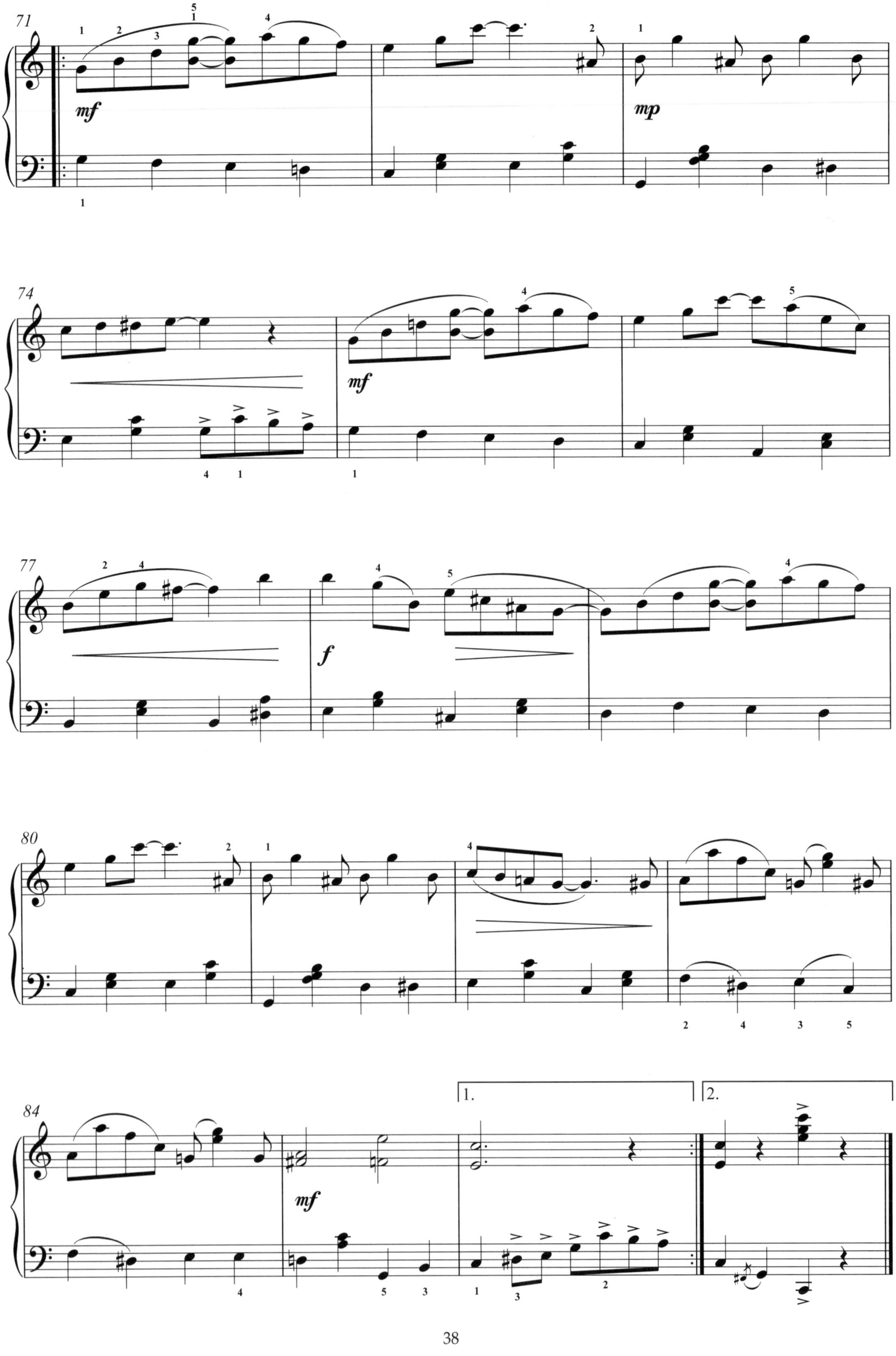
71
mf
mp
74
mf
77
f
80
84
1.
2.
mf

Peacherine Rag

Composed by Scott Joplin

Maple Leaf Rag

Composed by Scott Joplin

A steady march tempo

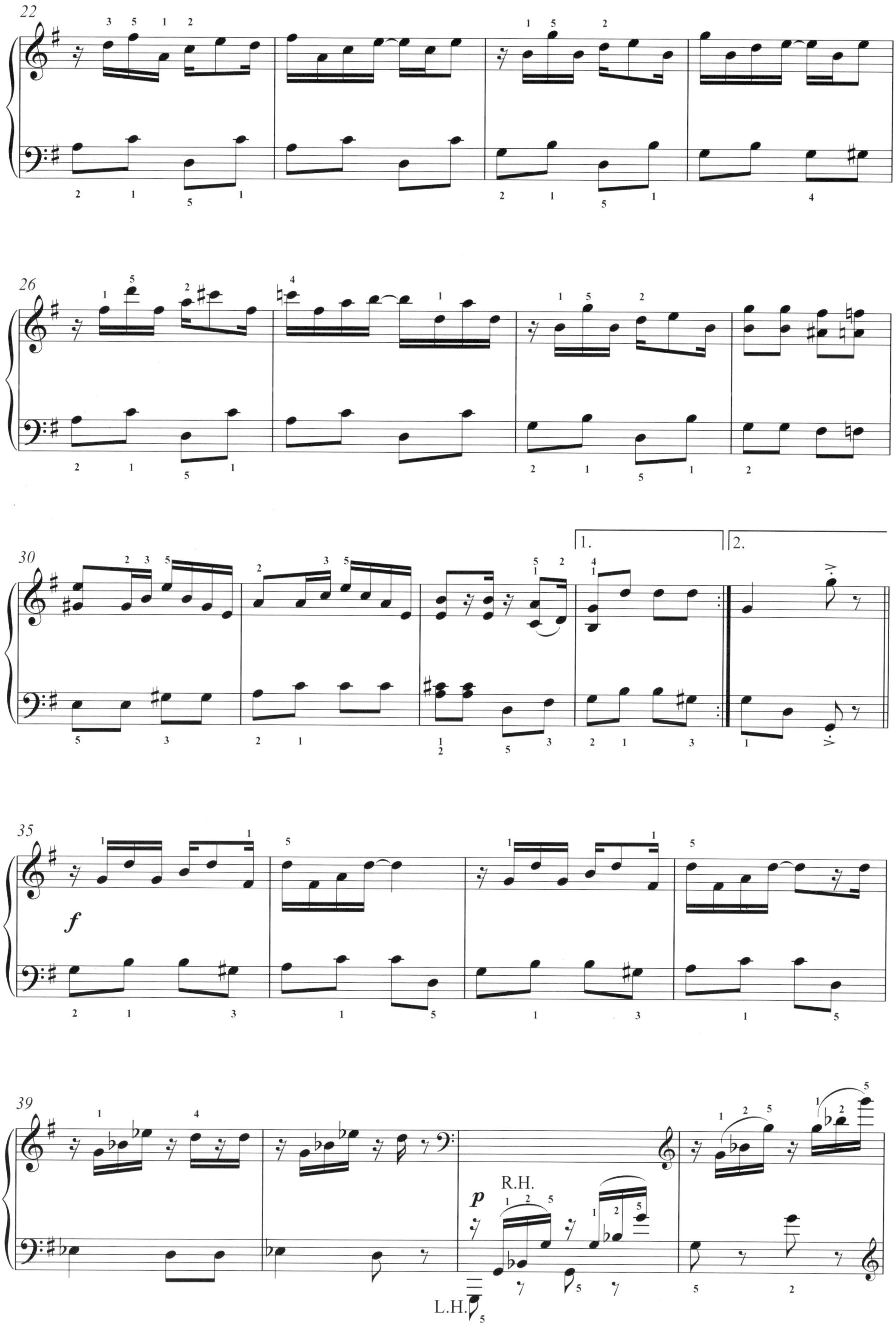
1.
2.
R.H.
L.H.

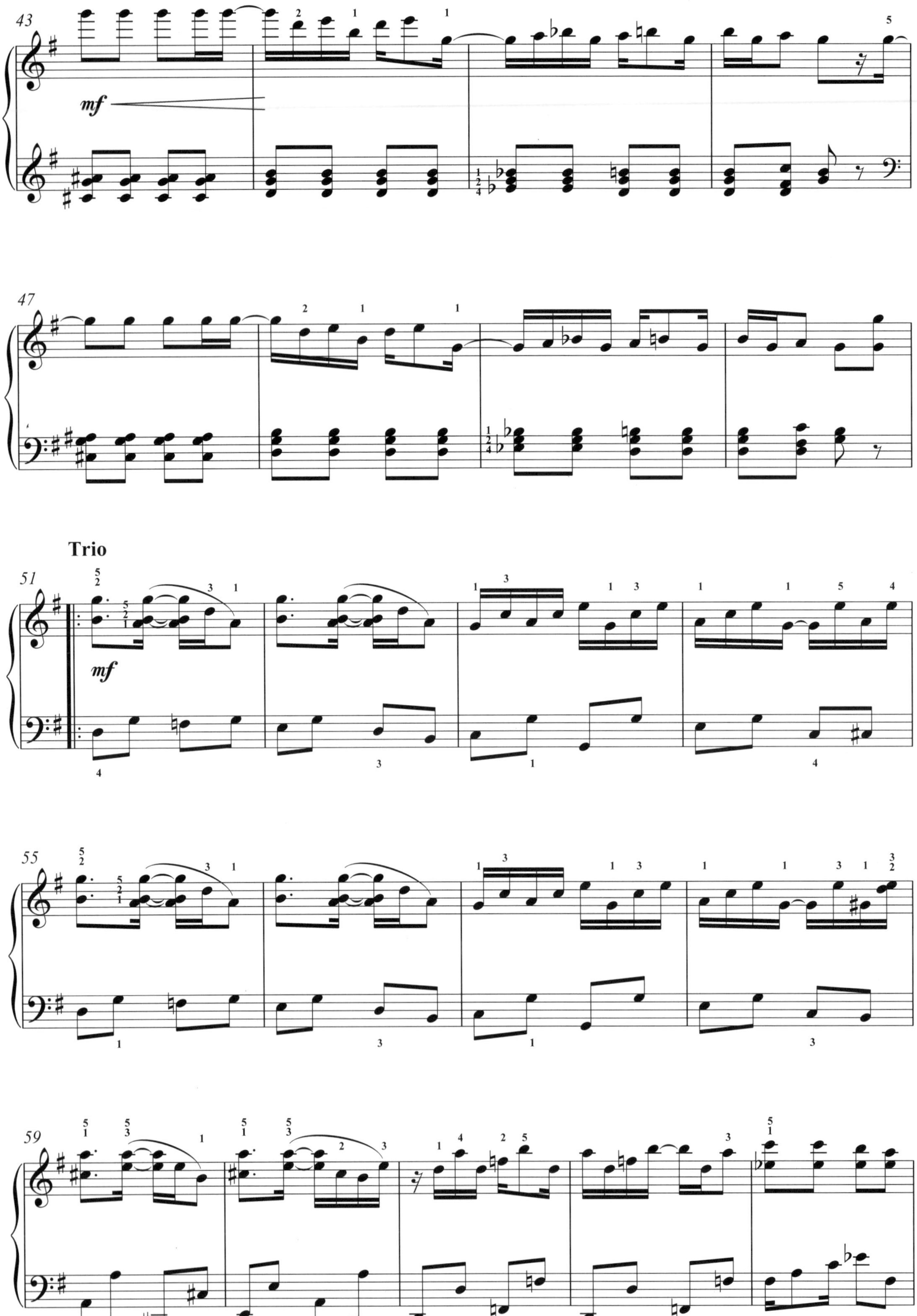
Trio
mf

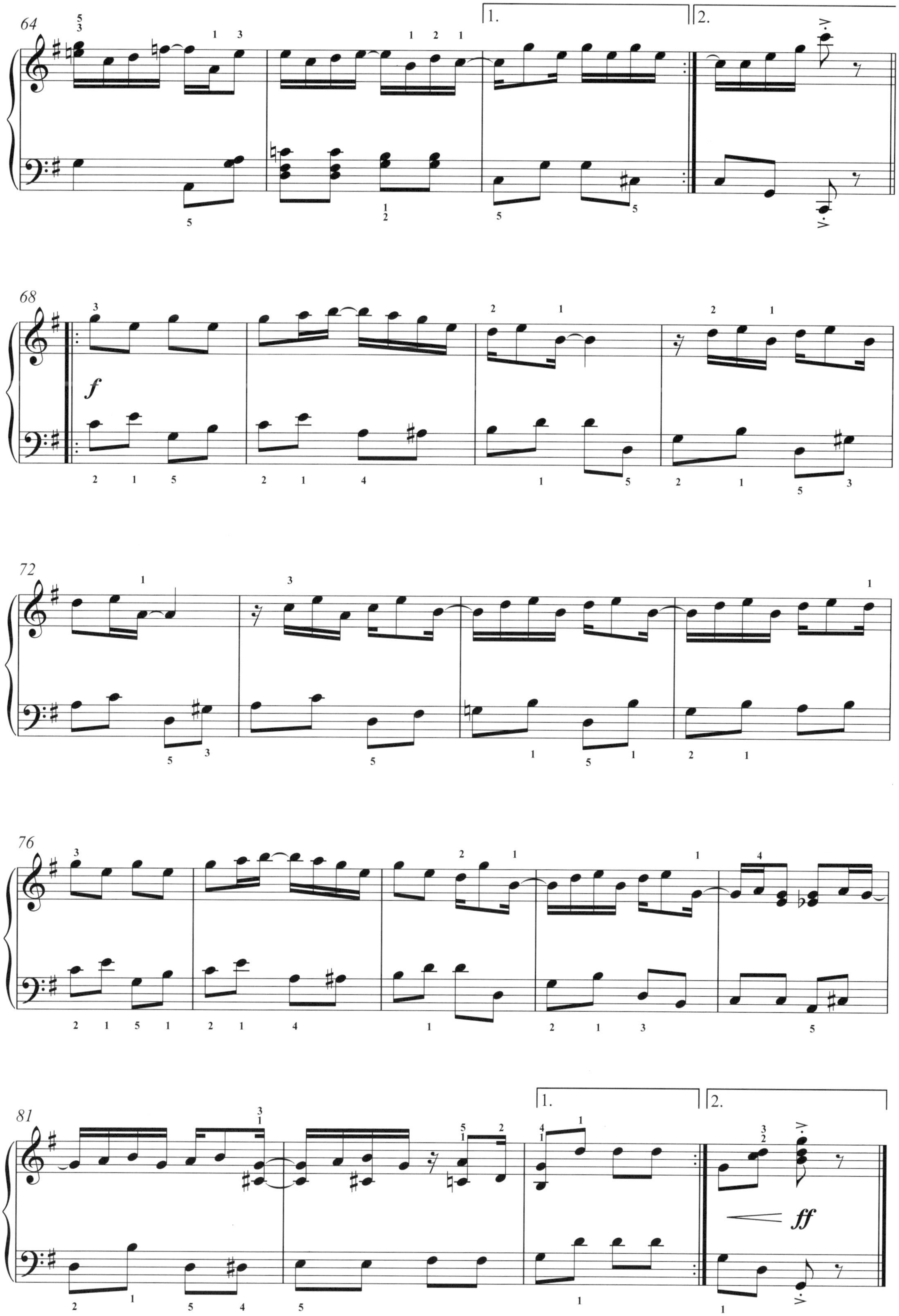

Original Rags

Composed by Scott Joplin

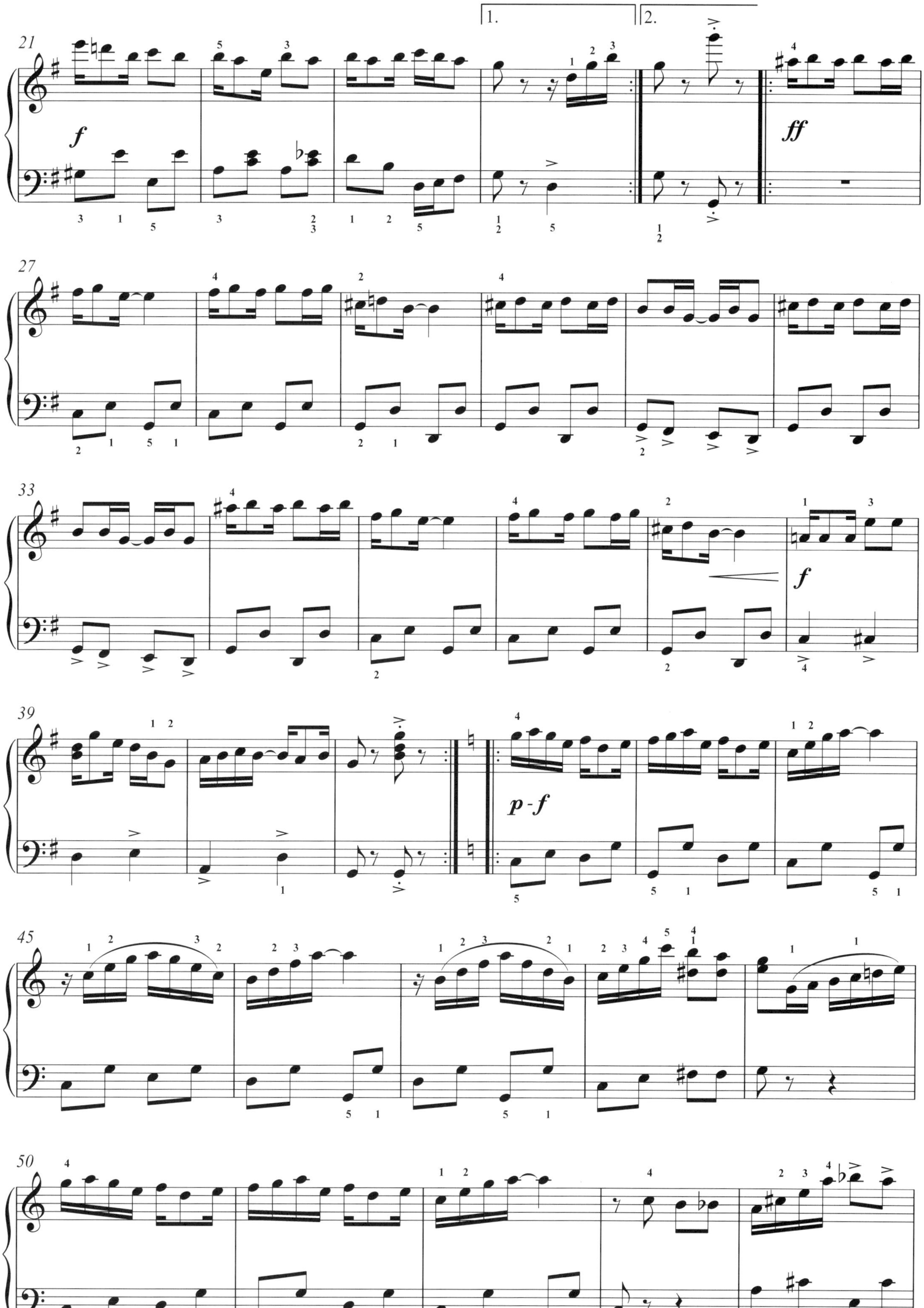
21
1.
2.
f
ff
27
33
f
39
p - f
45
50

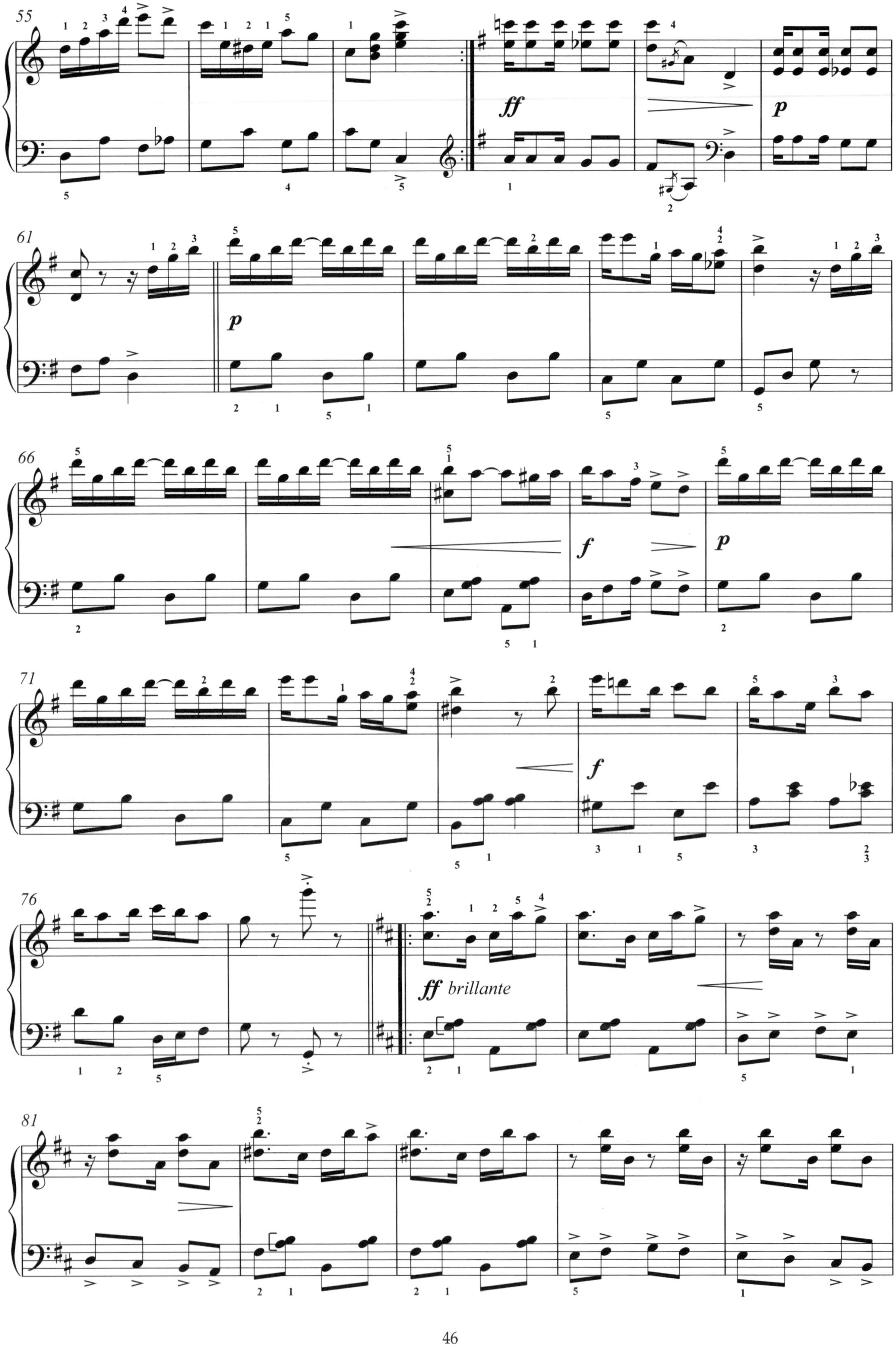
55
ff
p
61
p
66
f
p
71
f
76
ff brillante
81

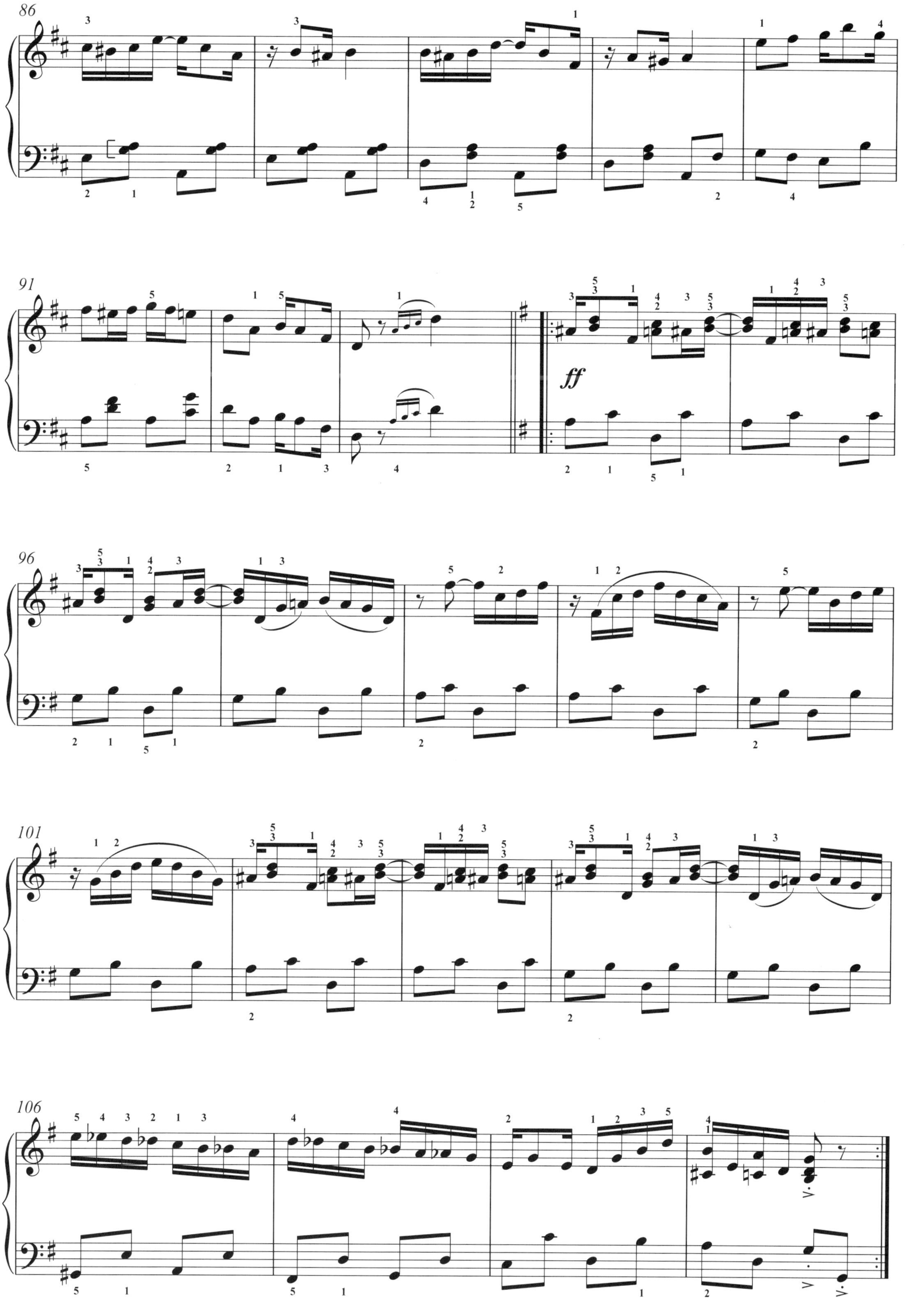
86
91
ff
96
101
106

Palm Leaf Rag

Composed by Scott Joplin

This arrangement © Copyright 2006 Boston Music Company.
All Rights Reserved. International Copyright Secured.

Moderately

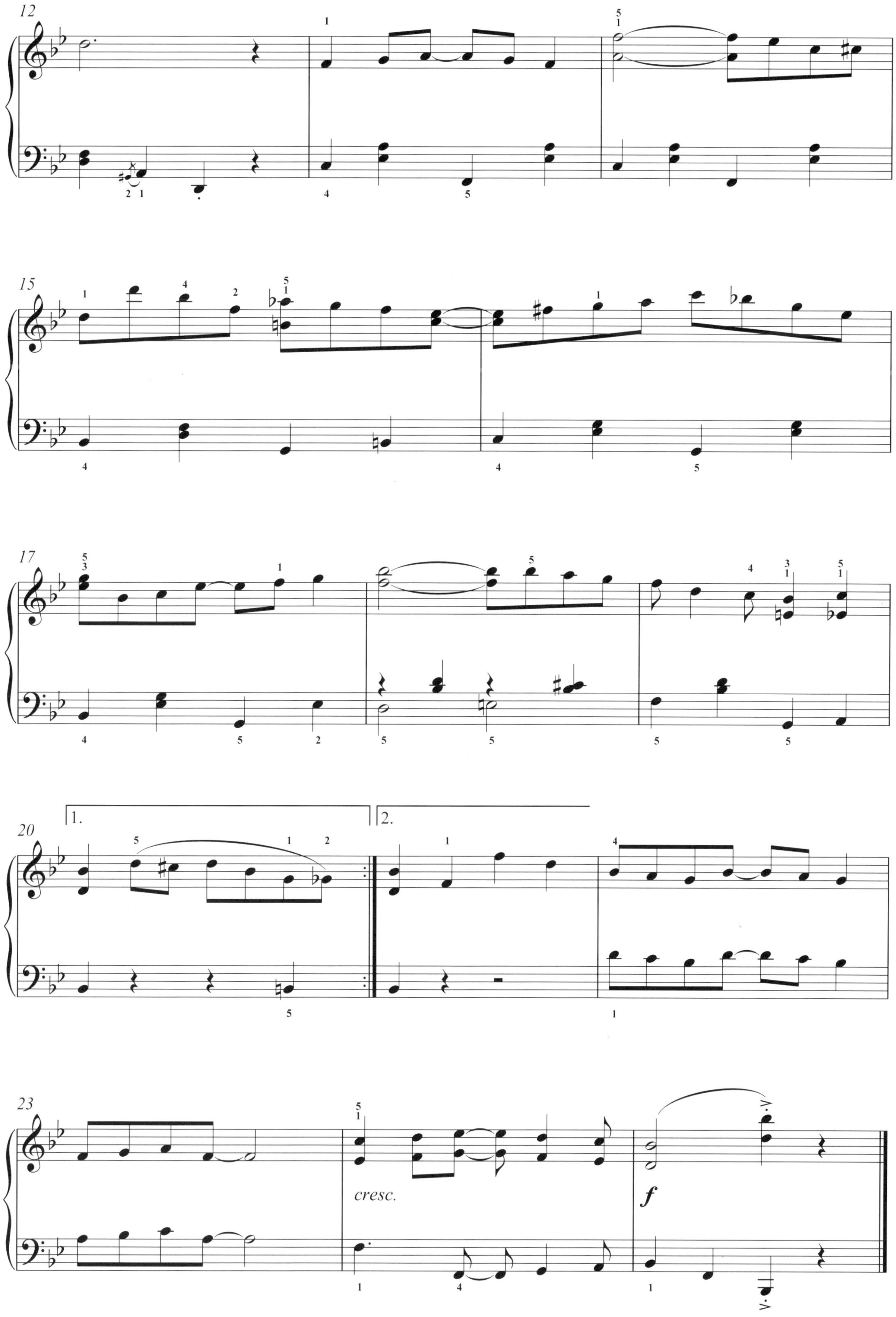
1.
2.
cresc.
f

Pine Apple Rag

Composed by Scott Joplin

© Copyright 2008 Dorsey Brothers Music Limited.
All Rights Reserved. International Copyright Secured.

Slow march tempo

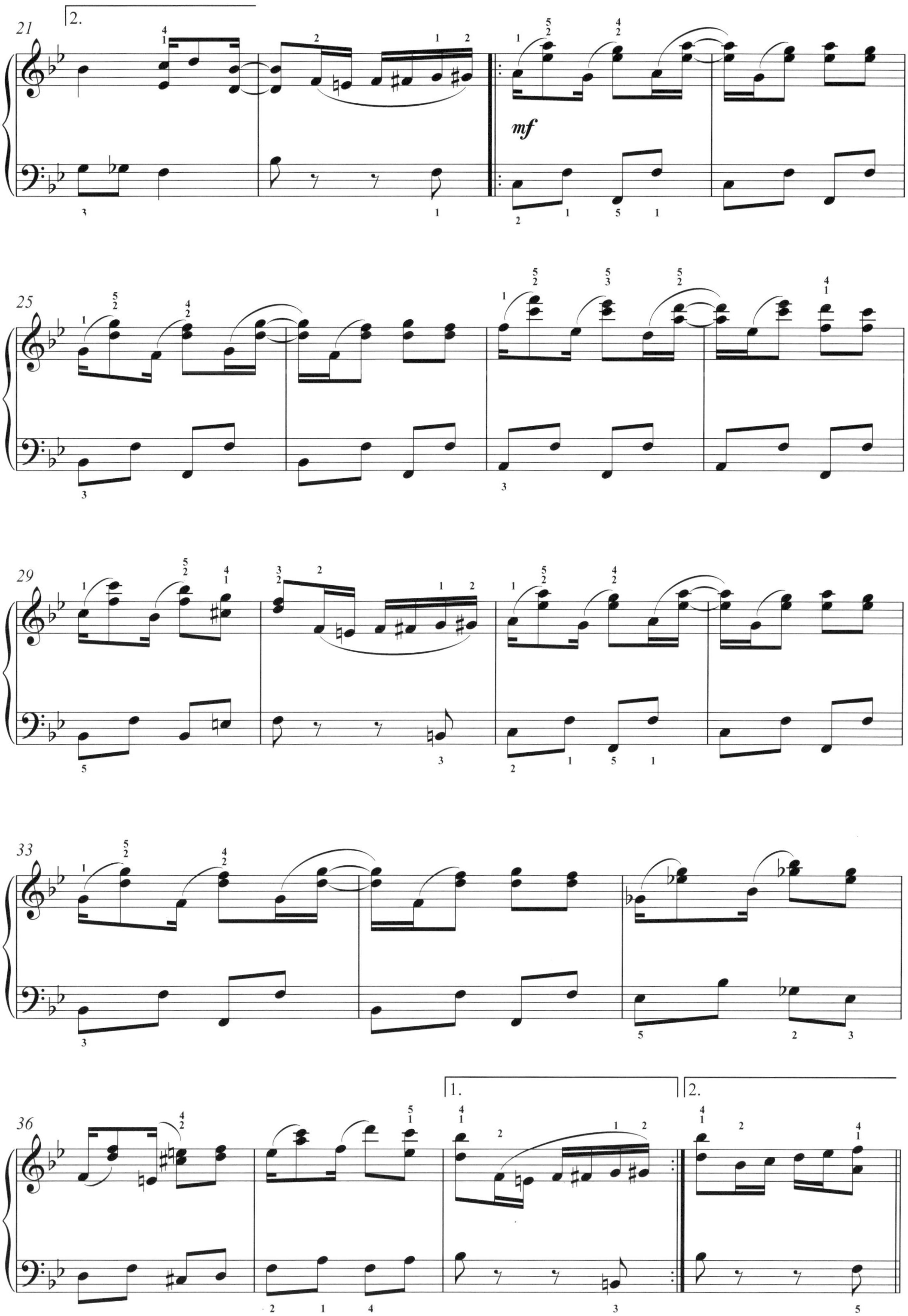
21
2.
mf
25
29
33
36
1.
2.

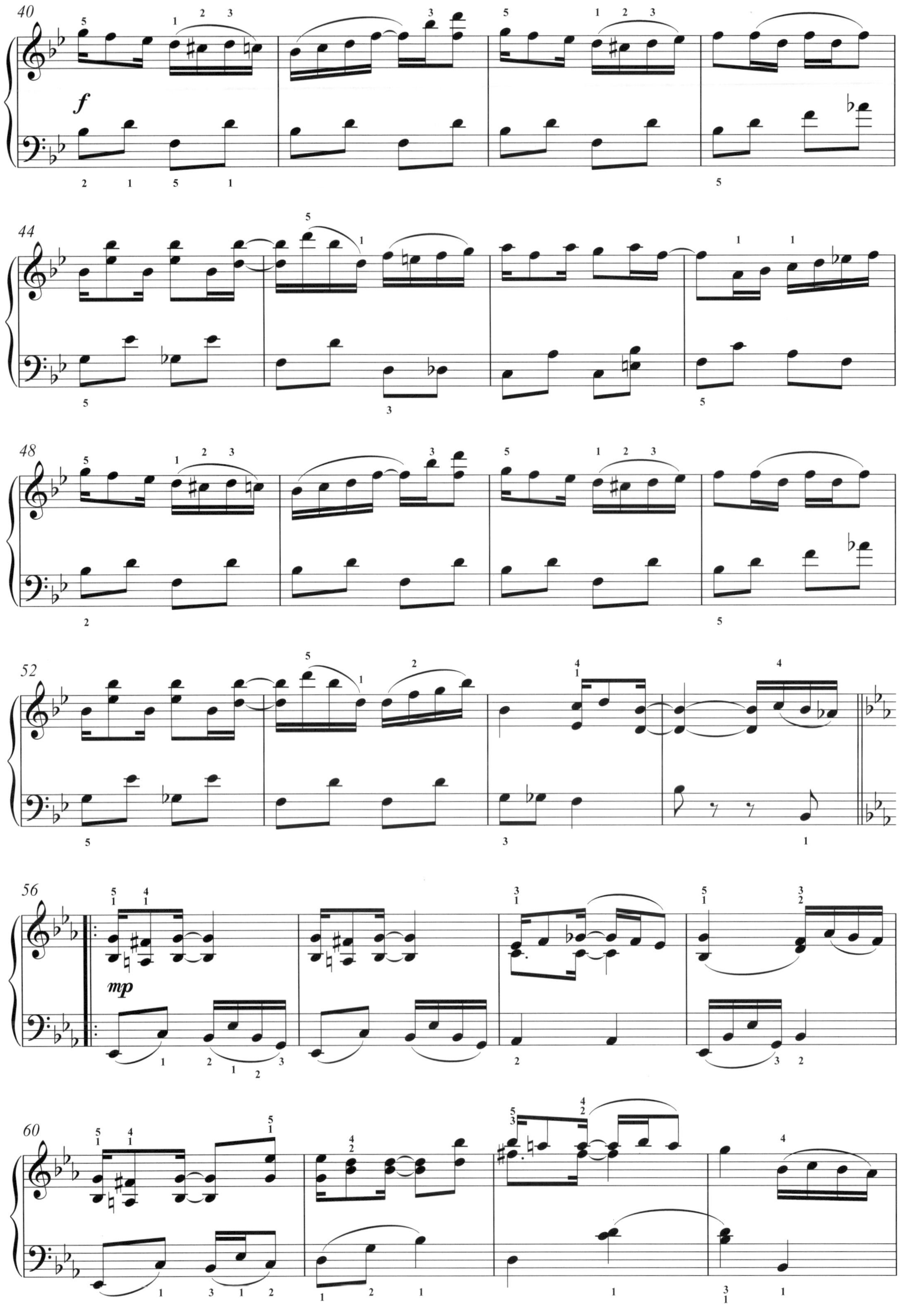
40
f
44
48
52
56
mp
60

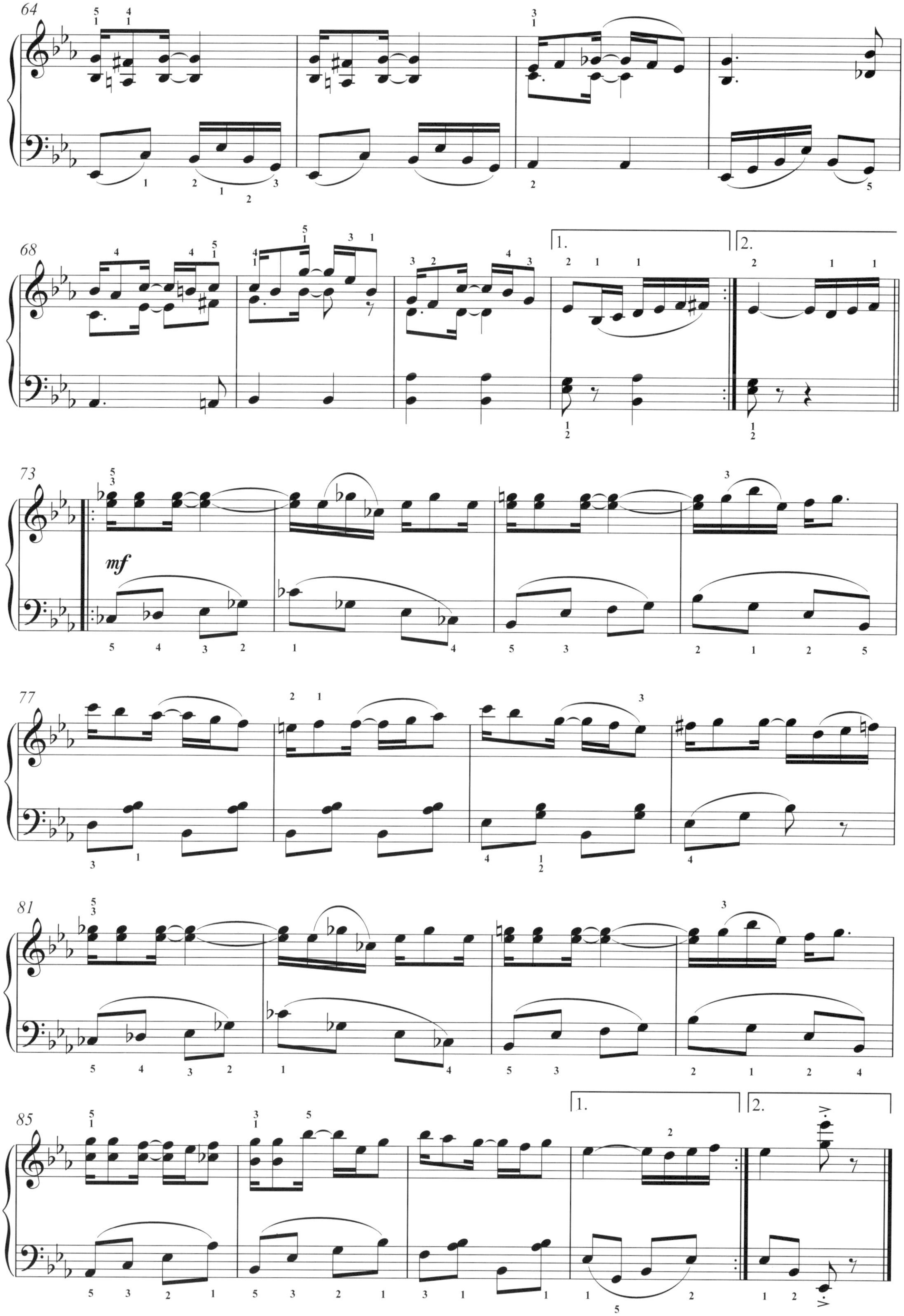
64
68
1.
2.
73
mf
77
81
85
1.
2.

Ragtime Dance

Composed by Scott Joplin

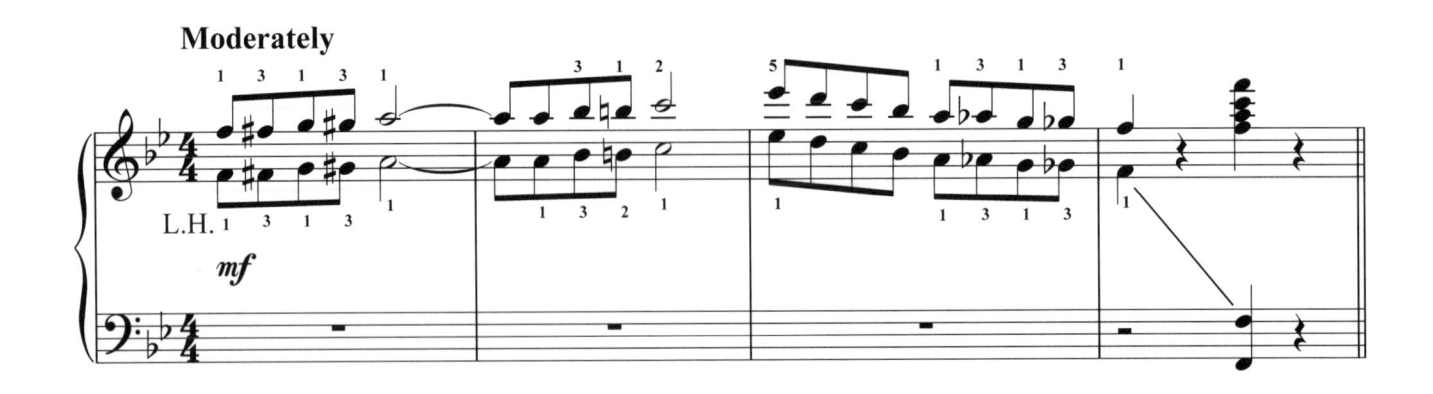

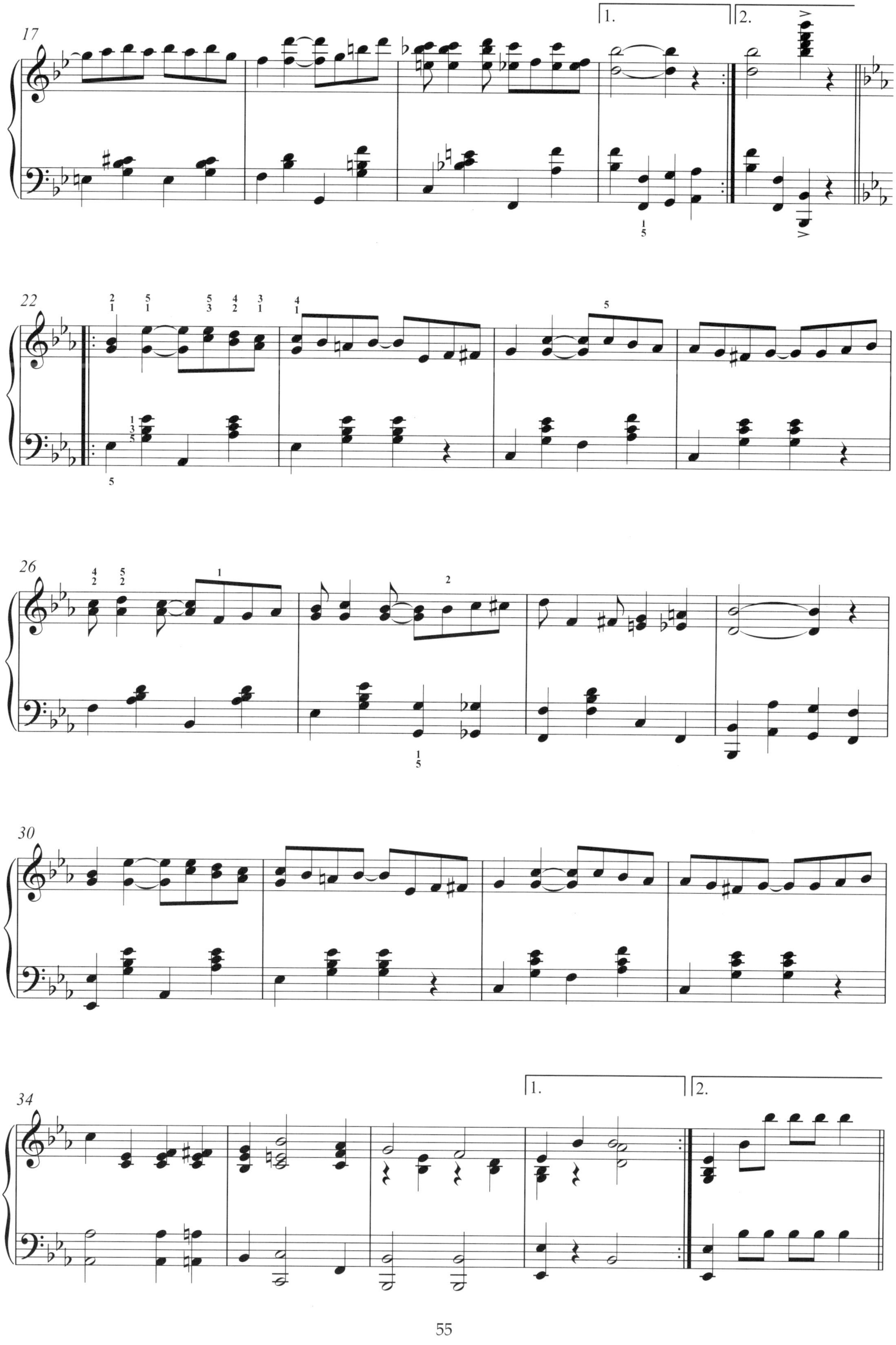
17
1.
2.
22
26
30
34
1.
2.

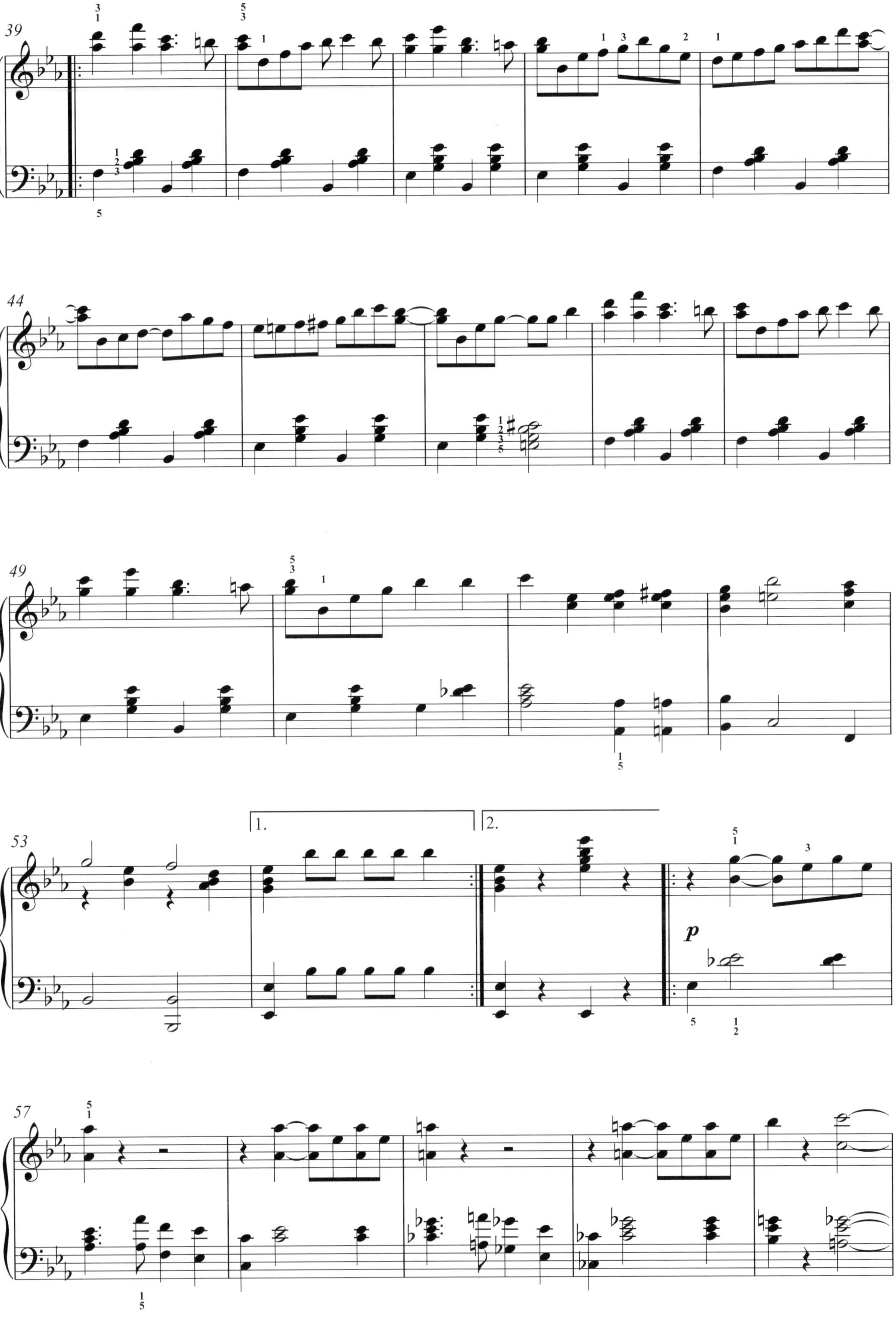
39
44
49
53
1.
2.
p
57

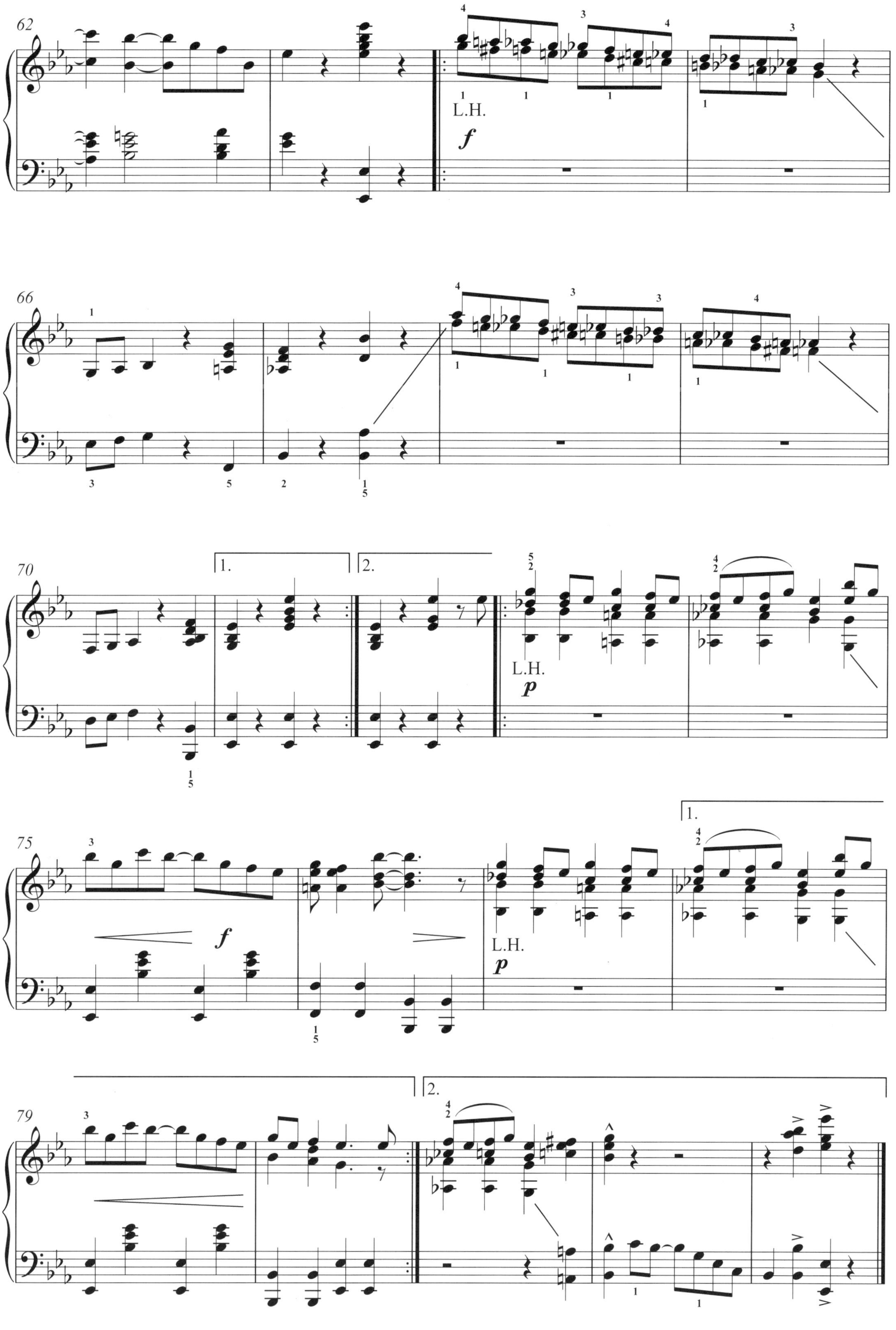
62
L.H.
f
66
70
1.
2.
L.H.
p
75
f
1.
L.H.
p
79
2.

Weeping Willow

Composed by Scott Joplin

This arrangement © Copyright 2006 Boston Music Company.
All Rights Reserved. International Copyright Secured.

59

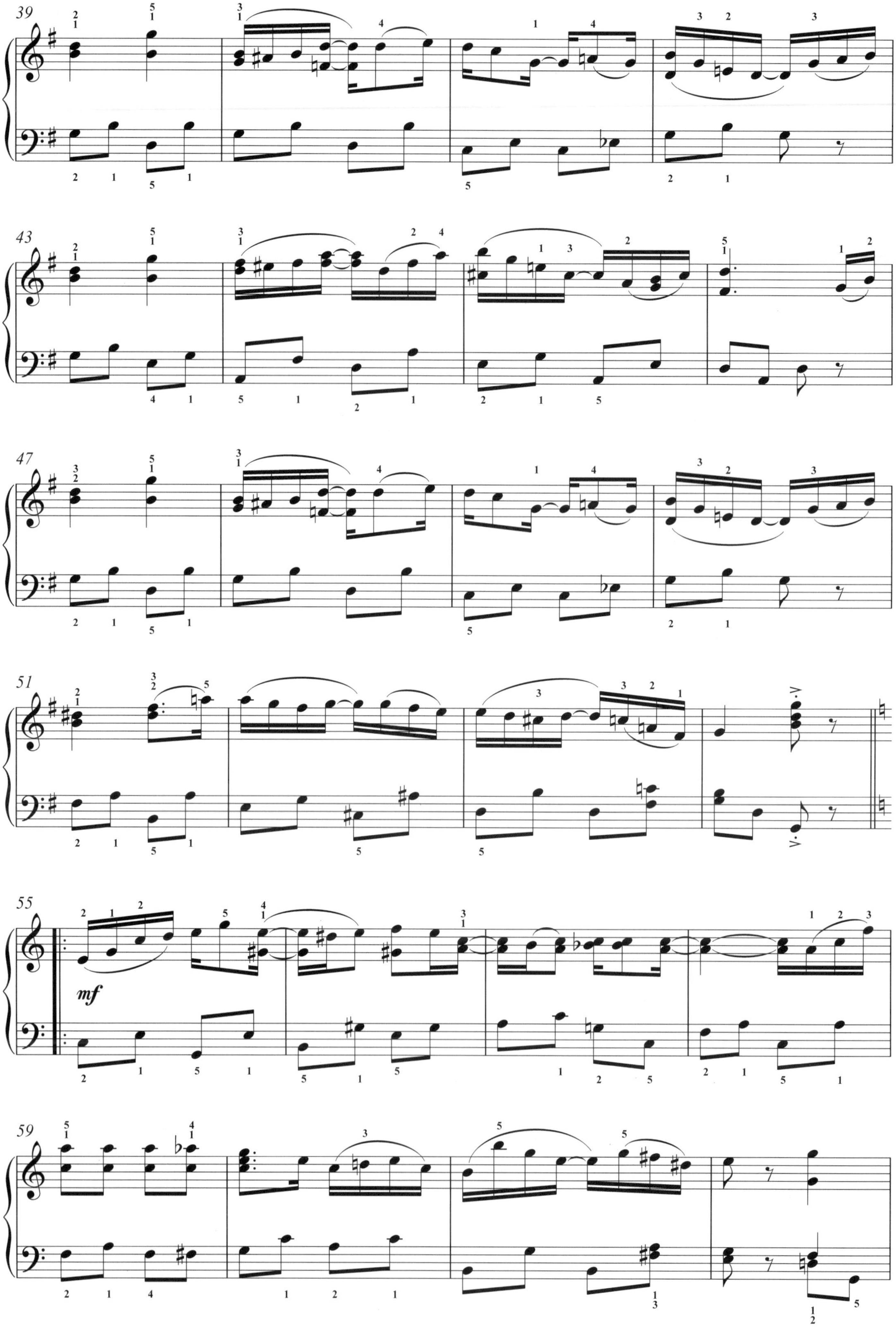
mf

61

The Strenuous Life

Composed by Scott Joplin

This arrangement © Copyright 1974 Yorktown Music Press, Inc. (ASCAP).
All Rights Reserved. International Copyright Secured.

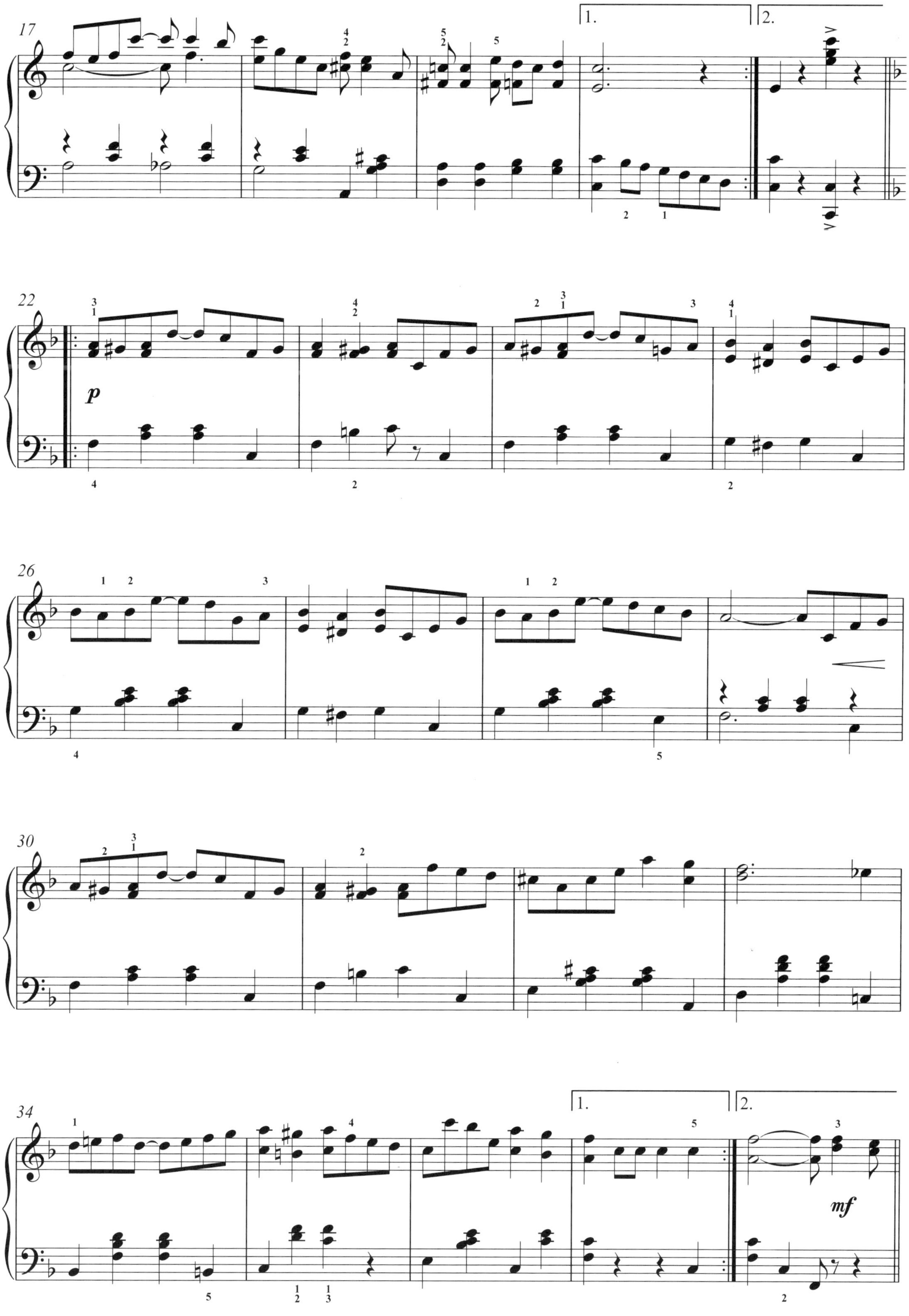
17
1.
2.
22
p
26
30
34
1.
2.
mf

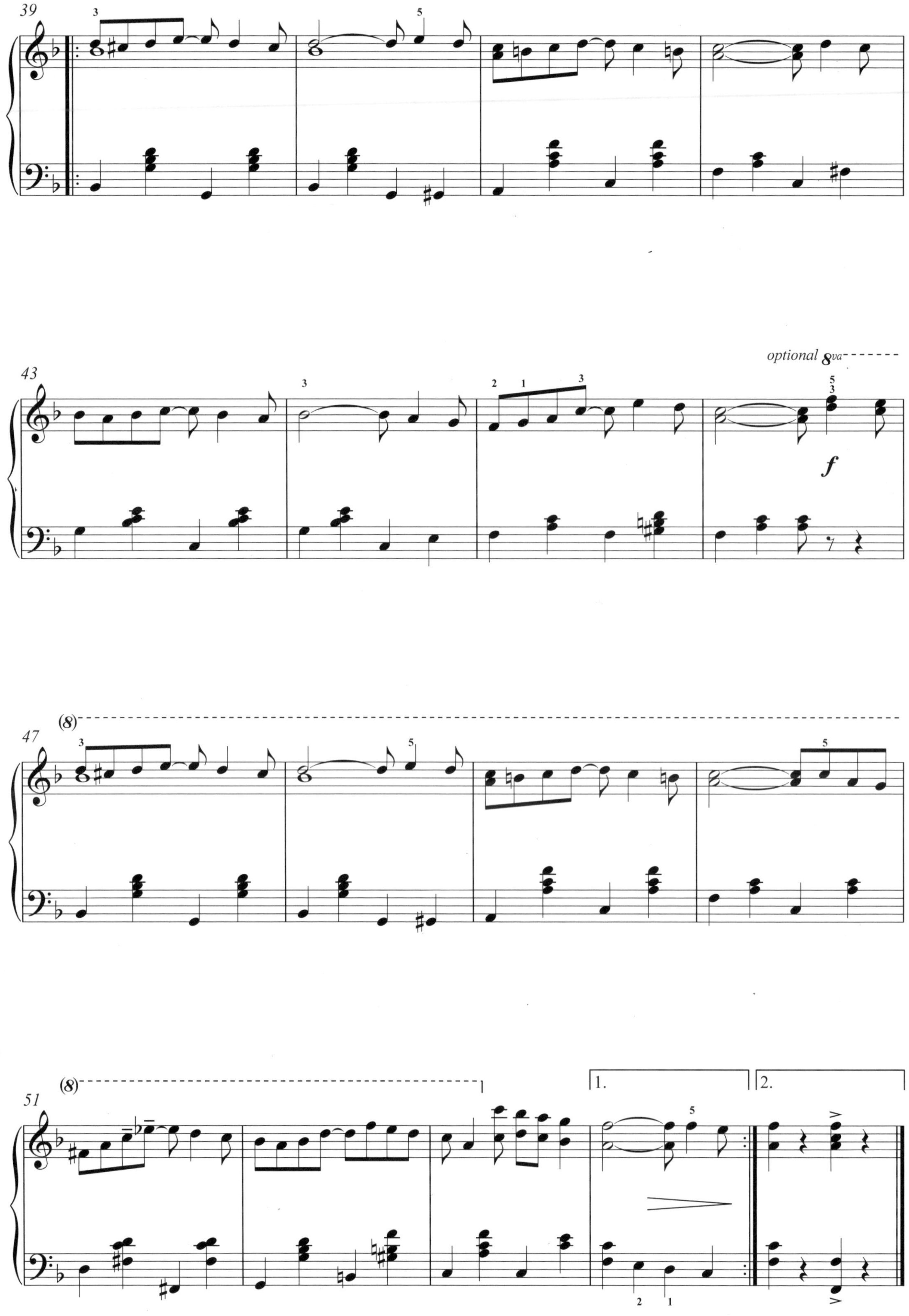

1 2 3 4 5 6 7 8 9